Inspirations

journal belongs to...

© 2016 Ranch House Press
All rights reserved. Printed in the United States of America.

www.annettebridges.com

ISBN: 978-0-9981576-8-9

Journal Prompts

1. What song lyrics especially move you?
2. Build a list of quotations that resonate with you every time you read them.
3. Paste photographs of places you've visited that gazing at the setting gives you feelings of serenity. Write about how you felt when you there. Try to recreate the scene in your mind and paint the picture with words.
4. Create a collage of magazine images that ignites your joy.
5. Begin a word bank that defines what it means to inspire and be inspired.
6. What inspires YOU? What down the FIRST things that come to your mind.
7. Recount a story of courage and conviction that has influenced you.
8. What books, movies or people motivate you to act bravely?
9. Describe something you do in your life that really excites you -- which you especially enjoy and most love to do.
10. Have you always followed your intuition? Write about a time you're thankful you followed your intuition as well as about a time when you wish you had.
11. What is your inner voice telling you right now?
12. Give yourself a pep talk today and write as many sentences as your heart guides that begin with "I can…"
13. What are the beliefs you cherish with all of your heart regardless of what anyone else says or what the evidence may even be to the contrary. Write your statements of strong beliefs. Begin with "I believe…"
14. Spend today avoiding bad news in newspapers, television or the Internet. Keep your focus on looking for GOOD news stories and write about something that especially moved you today.
15. Do something every day that encourages you in some way. Keep a record of everything - even the smallest thing you do or an experience you have or witness that warms your heart. Then when you're having a day when inspiration feels sparse you'll have a list to assure your hope for better days.
16. What words of encouragement would you give to someone who has lost hope? Read it to yourself when YOU need it.
17. What makes you tick? Gives you renewed energy? Lifts you up? Boosts your spirit?
18. Where do you find refuge?
19. Name what you need daily, weekly and monthly to feel like yourself. What fills you up enough to handle what life brings?
20. Jot down ten activities that TRULY renew you.
21. When you're stressed it can be hard to remember the good times. Prep your heart by recalling in full sensory detail ten feel-good moments that made you peaceful, relaxed or happy.
22. A bucket list is about once in a lifetime adventure. A thimble list, on the other hand, is about all the tiny thrills and simple pleasures you want to experience often. Write your thimble list.
23. Make a list of sentences and phrases that would brighten your day. Buy a pack of sticky notes and write a group of inspiring messages from your list. Leave your notes around town – on a door, above a water fountain, inside a book and so on. Experience the joy of sharing words of inspiration and encouragement.
24. What are five "leaps" you've made in your life toward new horizons whether or not the leap turned out in your favor? What matters is paying attention to where and why you leaped in the first place.
25. How has a failure or a setback helped you develop a new talent, skill or interest? Reflect on and appreciate the talents that you've mined from unexpected life challenges.
26. As you go through your day, be aware of what things you would keep doing, no matter what. Write them down to appreciate what truly matters to you.
27. Interview five people you trust – by email, by phone or in person. Ask them: What do you count on me for? Where and when do I seem most passionate? What do I bring to your life? This will reveal gifts you might not otherwise see. Appreciate yourself reflected in the eyes of those who know you best.
28. Ask yourself: What action would I take on one of my goals if my life were "normal" right now? Write down the possibilities. Be open to surprise.
29. You can increase your happiness when you pause for thirty seconds to savor good moments using all of your senses. Focus on smelling, tasting, touching and relishing in what's delightful. Such as, linger in the warmth of a hug or bask in the adoration in your pet's eyes. Every time you do this, you are literally writing your brain for greater joy.
30. Who are your role models? Write down the names of your heroes, whether they are personal friends or famous leaders.

color your world

ABOUT the CREATOR

Annette Bridges is an author, publisher and women's retreat host on a mission to help every woman realize her story is extraordinary, valuable and noteworthy.

She has published the ***Color Your World Journal Series*** and formed a journal club to provide community, support and tools for women to record their ideas, feelings, experiences, memories and all the important details of their lives.

Before writing books and publishing journals and coloring books, this former public school and homeschool educator spent a decade writing hundreds of helpful, instructive, and light-hearted columns published by Texas newspapers, parenting magazines, websites and bloggers.

Annette lives on a Texas cattle ranch with her husband John, dachshund Lady and lots of cows. She can drive a tractor but only if wearing a fresh coat of lipstick and it's not her pedicure day!

You can learn more about Annette's books and products, blogs and videos as well as her women's retreats and other events at www.annettebridges.com.

Look for her on social media, too!

MESSAGE from the PUBLISHER

The *Color Your World Journal Series* is a pathway to self-discovery. It's where you write notes to yourself. Be your own cheerleader. Give yourself encouragement. Tell yourself what you're grateful for. Celebrate you!

There are countless reasons to keep a journal including collecting favorite recipes, listing goals and celebrating every experience and every one that's near and dear to you. A journal provides a home for the memories and lessons learned that you never want to forget.

Why a niche journal?

If you're anything like me, you have a journal (or even two or three journals) where you write anything and everything about anything and everything. My challenge comes when trying to find something I've written. I flip and flip through the pages of my two, three or four journals trying to find whatever it is. I never remember which journal I wrote down my whatever's!!

The solution? A niche journal! A journal that has a specific focus and theme! A journal where you can record your ideas, inspirations and things you want to remember in the appropriate journal.

Why big unlined paper?

Because big unlined paper is needed to record big ideas, dreams and memories! You need room to grow, stretch and expand. You need space to think beyond the confines of what you've always done, to pursue new dreams, discover your power and reimagine your purpose again and again. You need pages without lines and limitations to reconnect with your creative, perfectly imperfect self.

Plus, big unlined paper gives you space for more than words. You have plenty of room to doodle, draw or post photographs and clippings, too.

Why color is important?

When you journal, use colored pens and markers! Your world doesn't happen in black and white. Your life should be lived and written about in many colors. Even dark and sad memories feel lighter and brighter when told in color.

Journaling in color affects your mood and perception of your world. Colors evoke calm, cheer and comfort. Using color can lift your spirit and inspire your imagination. You may be surprised by all the beautiful benefits from adding more color into your life story.

When journaling, give yourself time to listen to your heart and reflect. Breathe in the moments. Feel. Be quiet. Let yourself be totally and thoroughly present with your thoughts. Let your heart transform you and teach you new insights. Open your mind to consider new ideas and possibilities. You may find that what your heart teaches will be life changing.